LABOUR, LANCASHIRE AND THE 1924 GOVERNMENT: ITS RISE, FALL AND PARALLELS WITH TODAY

Hugh Gault

Gretton Books
Cambridge

First published in 2024 by Gretton Books

© Hugh Gault 2024

The moral right of Hugh Gault to be identified as the author of this work has been asserted in accordance with the Copyright, Design and Patents Act 1988

All rights reserved. Apart from any use permitted under UK copyright law no part of this publication may be reproduced, stored in a retrieval system, or transmitted, in any form or by any means without the prior written permission of the publisher, nor be otherwise circulated in any form of binding or cover other than that in which it is published and without a similar condition being imposed on the subsequent purchaser.

A CIP catalogue record for this title is available from the British Library.

ISBN   978-1-7392067-8-9

Printed and bound by 4edge in the UK

CONTENTS

Summary	iv
Introduction	1
Why Lancashire?	2
Composition of the 1924 Labour government	5
Lancashire politics in the 1920s	14
Lancashire MPs in the Cabinet	19
The 1924 Labour government in office	30
Parallels with today	38
Appendix	40

SUMMARY

The first Labour government led by Ramsay MacDonald was ushered into power by Baldwin's resignation and Asquith's acquiescence. It was expected to fail.

After the 1923 general election Labour was the strongest party in Lancashire, with one-tenth of the party's MPs overall and a Cabinet core comprising five MPs with Lancashire constituencies. Three (Philip Snowden, JR Clynes and Arthur Henderson) are well-known; Stephen Walsh and Tom Shaw had entered parliament via the mining and weaving trade unions, and were Secretary for War and Minister of Labour respectively. All five were from working-class backgrounds, most had left school by the age of twelve and all before they were fifteen. Three represented areas where they had close local connections.

MacDonald's government avoided extreme socialist measures, with Wheatley's Housing Act their only significant legislative success. They did little to tackle increasing unemployment. MacDonald came under attack, both personally and for the withdrawal of the *Workers' Weekly* prosecution. Labour lost a censure vote over the latter and resigned. In the 1924 general election Labour's credibility was further damaged but their vote increased, replacing the Liberals as the main party of opposition to a revived Conservative party, now with two-thirds of the Commons seats.

A century later the parallels with today are striking. For example, being in government does not automatically result in progress; the scope for action is constrained by events, legacy and public opinion; and one person's free speech may offend somebody else.

INTRODUCTION

A leading article in the *Guardian* in November 2023 judged that 'Politics now looks like the 19th century, where two major parties, led by the higher castes, vie for the votes of a marginalised working class'.[1] Leaving aside the question of whether many of the 'marginalised working class' could actually vote in the 19th century, there may be an issue for today's Labour party if it no longer represents its social base. It is too facile to accept that politics and political representation are now professionalised, with lawyers to the fore, especially when respondents to opinion surveys regularly complain of being treated as electoral fodder and being taken for granted. To some minds it was people reacting to being overlooked, their views discarded, by professional politicians that led to the marginal vote in the 2016 Brexit referendum to leave the European Union. If this analysis is correct, people not only objected but decided to let politicians know.

By contrast with the *Guardian* judgement, it was very clear in 1924 that Labour politicians were of a similar background to their constituents, frequently having grown up alongside them and in some cases representing the area they were born in. Perhaps this made politics more local, even parochial; arguably, however, it ensured that politicians were in touch with, and in many cases had experienced for themselves, the issues that mattered to their constituents. This would be likely to go beyond today's 'awareness' of their concerns to foster an enlightened understanding and, ideally, empathy.

---

[1] *Guardian* 4 November 2023

The Labour Party developed from the trades union movement via the Independent Labour Party (ILP), Labour Representation Committee (LRC) and other groups that sought to bring working class concerns to the fore (the Social Democratic Foundation, the *Clarion* newspaper and cycling club, and William Morris' Socialists, to name but a few). These groups were most prominent from the 1880s through to the early twentieth century, amplified by an increasing interest in Communism. To caricature the extremes: while right-wing Conservativism would stress the individual's personal responsibility and self-reliance (and the infallibility of markets of course), left-wing socialists would see community, and the situation in which individuals lived, their circumstances, as fundamental. One-nation Tories and 'New Labour' would fall between these two poles. Hence the significance of the oft-quoted, 'There is no such thing as society' and the ire it aroused at the time and since. Thatcher was not just affirming her political stance but trashing those views that opposed her.

WHY LANCASHIRE?

The major working-class occupations in the 19th century were agriculture, construction, mining, weaving and cotton mills, and transport, particularly railways, shipping and the docks. These are the occupations more readily organised, though not exclusively men's. Women featured, often predominantly, among mill workforces but their sisters were as likely to be in domestic service or undertaking out-work from home. Dispersed occupations by their nature defy unionisation to the same degree.

There would of course be many others, such as the developing utilities (gas, water and sewage), other manufacturing industries or warehousing, but the numbers employed would be substantially less.

Even the significance of agriculture was declining as people moved for work into the built-up areas.

London would have had some of these occupations but not all would be at scale, and agriculture and mining in particular would be confined to the periphery (the Kent coalfield, for example). All of them, however, would have been evident in Lancashire, with Liverpool docks second only to London, and Manchester known as 'cottonopolis'. Even areas such as Rossendale combined weaving with agriculture, often carried out by the same people who thrived (or survived) by diversification.[2] Rawtenstall was known for its jute. There were 108 collieries in Lancashire when the mines were nationalised in 1947, largely between Colne and Blackburn in the north and around Wigan in the south.

In 1923 615 seats were contested in the October general election called by the Conservative Prime Minister Stanley Baldwin on a matter of principle. Although the Conservatives remained the largest party, winning 258 seats, this was a net reduction of 86 from the 344 seats they held previously.[3] The Labour Party and the Liberals received fewer votes (about 30% each compared to 38% for the Conservatives), but the distribution of votes favoured Labour with 191 seats compared to a combined 158 for the Liberal factions led by Asquith and Lloyd George. Overall the Liberals had a net gain of 43 seats and Labour 49. The first Labour government, a minority one, was eventually formed towards the end of January 1924 after the Conservatives lost by 72 on an amendment

---

[2] GH Tupling, *The Economic History of Rossendale* with a new introduction by RC Richardson (Lancaster, 2022)

[3] House of Commons Library Research Briefing, *UK Election Statistics: 1918-1923, A Long Century of Elections* (London, 2023), 17

moved by Labour in reply to the King's speech at the opening of the 1924 parliament. Baldwin resigned and MacDonald accepted the King's summons to form a government.

Only eight of the 615 MPs were women. In March 1917 women's suffrage (for those over 30) was approved by the Commons for parliamentary elections[4] and in the 1918 election the first woman MP was elected.[5] The first women Labour MPs were Margaret Bondfield, Dorothea Jewson and Susan Lawrence, all elected at the December 1923 general election. All three lost their seats a year later, though Bondfield and Lawrence returned to parliament in 1926. Meanwhile, Ellen Wilkinson had been elected in 1924.

Labour's 191 MPs were spread across the country in a way that contrasts notably with the position today. In 1923 32.7% of Londoners voted Labour, but the party won only one-seventh of the London seats.[6] In other cities with a population of more than half a million (Birmingham, Glasgow, Manchester, Sheffield and Liverpool),[7] 37% of the votes went to Labour, resulting in almost a third of the seats (32.7%). However, less than 10% of the parliamentary party came from these cities, the lowest at any election in this period apart from 1918 and 1931 (and both of these

---

[4] Women householders had been able to vote in municipal elections for some time. It would be 1928 before the parliamentary franchise was equalised for men and women at 21.

[5] Constance Markievicz (Sinn Fein) though she did not take her seat; the first woman to do so was Nancy Astor (Conservative) after a 1919 by-election. Women in the House of Commons - UK Parliament - accessed 27 November 2023

[6] Frank Bealey and Michael Dyer, 'Size of place and the Labour vote in Britain, 1918-1966', *Western Political Quarterly*, 24 (1971), 84-113

[7] Leeds' population growth brought it into this group from 1945.

had very particular circumstances). Yet these large cities are the most fertile areas for Labour representation today.

COMPOSITION OF THE 1924 LABOUR GOVERNMENT

The centenary of the first Labour government has been widely trumpeted, with conferences held and many articles and books published. One of the first books to appear was Peter Clark's 'The Men of 1924'.[8] Clark's book opens with a striking first paragraph:

> In January 1924 a British government was formed with a Cabinet consisting of twenty white men in dark suits of Christian background, with an average age of fifty-seven. They succeeded a Cabinet consisting of nineteen white men in dark suits of Christian background, with an average age of fifty-six. ... they were replaced by a Cabinet of twenty-one white men in dark suits of Christian background, with an average age of fifty-three.

Clark's next sentence begins 'And that is where the resemblances end ...' For indeed they do. What might have seemed on the surface to be continuation and conformity was belied by the diversity of MacDonald's government.

One issue that might be dealt with first is the size of the Cabinet, twenty according to Clark but twenty-three often reported at the time.[9]

---

[8] Peter Clark, *The Men of 1924: Britain's First Labour Government* (London, 2023) Others include David Torrance, *The Wild Men* (London, 2024) and Jon Cruddas, *A Century of Labour* (Cambridge, 2024)

[9] For example, 'The new British government', *Advocate of Peace Through Justice*, 86 (1924), 147

The two law officers (the Attorney-General Patrick Hastings and the Solicitor-General Henry Slesser) are mentioned only in passing by Clark, while he does not include Frederick Roberts, the Minister of Pensions at all. Omitting the first two is unexceptionable as the law officers are at best semi-detached from their ministerial colleagues, understandably so, and in many governments the Solicitor-General would not be at Cabinet level - or at best might have observer status. The omission of any detail about the MP for West Bromwich, Frederick Roberts, is harder to explain and seems to be due to the absence of readily available source material.[10] Roberts at 48 was one of the younger members of the Cabinet and would be West Bromwich's MP for nineteen of the twenty-three years between 1918 and his death in 1941.[11] Pensions was a critical issue, old age pensions having been introduced in embryonic form by Lloyd George as recently as 1908 and pensions for disabled First World War soldiers and the bereaved still raising strong emotions, exacerbated by the hard economic times the country went through in the early 1920s.

MacDonald's Cabinet comprised five members, or more than one fifth, in the House of Lords (Haldane, Parmoor, Chelmsford, Thomson and Olivier). The first two had been MPs previously, Haldane as a Liberal and now Labour's Lord Chancellor, and Stafford Cripps' father Parmoor (Lord

---

[10] Even the Black Country History Archive holds only one photograph: Right Honourable F. O. Roberts M.P., Labour Member of Parliament for West Bromwich (blackcountryhistory.org) - accessed 23 November 2023. He has no entry in the Oxford Dictionary of National Biography.
There is some information, however, in Walter Smith (ed. Andrew Smith), *Born into Socialism* (Cambridge, 2022), 33-34

[11] Like several Labour colleagues he was out of parliament after the 1931 election which saw the formation of a Conservative-led 'national government', though initially with MacDonald as the nominal PM. Roberts was re-elected in 1935.

President of the Council). Chelmsford was also in the Lords already and became First Lord of the Admiralty. Thomson and Olivier were ennobled on 9 February 1924 as Baron Thomson of Cardington (in Bedfordshire), Secretary for Air, and Baron Olivier of Ramsden (in Oxfordshire), Secretary for India. By including so many in the Lords, MacDonald may have been signalling that his government would not be radical, or at least not so radical as to overturn the establishment. Disrupting the status quo was another matter. Or, as Maurice Cowling has put it,

> ... MacDonald aimed to produce a combination competent enough to command confidence, respectable enough to dispose of the accusation that the Labour Party was revolutionary and comprehensive enough to include anyone who might be dangerous outside.[12]

Two of the Cabinet were not in parliament at all at the government's formation: the Home Secretary Arthur Henderson had lost his Newcastle East seat in the 1923 election and had to wait for another to be found in Burnley. Henry Slesser only became an MP later in the year when he was elected for Leeds South-East.

Of the eighteen who were MPs and Cabinet members (including Henderson and Slesser), three were born in Lancashire (Clynes, Walsh and Shaw) and five represented Lancashire constituencies, including Henderson when he found a berth in Burnley. The other four were the three born there: JR Clynes, Deputy Leader of the Commons and Lord

---

[12] Maurice Cowling, *The Impact of Labour 1920-1924: The Beginning of Modern British Politics* (Cambridge, 1971), 366-367

Privy Seal, in Manchester North East (subsequently Platting),[13] the Secretary of War Stephen Walsh for Ince, and the Minister of Labour Tom Shaw in Preston. The other was Philip Snowden the Chancellor of the Exchequer for Colne Valley, but born across the border in Yorkshire.[14]

Two of the others represented Welsh constituencies (Ramsay MacDonald and Vernon Hartshorn, the Postmaster-General), two held Scottish seats (Willie Adamson the Secretary for Scotland and John Wheatley, Minister of Health) and three had their political base in the north-east (Sidney Webb for Seaham, Charles Trevelyan Newcastle Central and Patrick Hastings Wallsend).

Of the others, JH Thomas sat for Derby from 1910 to 1936, Josiah Wedgwood for Newcastle-under-Lyme, Staffordshire from 1906 to 1942, and Noel Buxton for North Norfolk - first as a Liberal from 1910 to 1918 and then for Labour from 1922 to 1930. Fred Jowett represented two Bradford constituencies, first West Bradford from 1906 to 1918 and then East Bradford, with stints there from 1922 to 1924 and 1929 to 1931, with Henry Slesser in Leeds South East from 1924 to 1929. Roberts' West Bromwich links have already been mentioned, and the others all had strong local connections (apart from Slesser) - often from birth. Even Buxton, Minister of Agriculture, had family connections to East Anglia.

Although several had started in the ILP, only Jowett remained so throughout his parliamentary career, resisting appeals from his colleagues to join the Labour Party itself. The ILP had a particular resonance in Bradford, of course, being the venue for the 1893 conference that

---

[13] Like Roberts he was out of parliament between 1931 and 1935.
[14] Snowden and Shaw both ceased to be MPs in 1931, the former then elevated to the Lords. Walsh died in 1929.

established it. Arguably, though, not strong enough to prevent Jowett's electoral defeat in 1924 and five years out of parliament.

Overall, therefore, almost one-third of the MPs in the 1924 Labour Cabinet had close, as well as current, Lancashire connections. Some further information on each of the MPs is tabulated in the Appendix.

Age

Apart from the absence of any women, one striking feature is the comparatively youthful profile of the Cabinet. Of the eighteen MPs, three were younger than 50, nine in their fifties and six in their sixties. The youngest was Slesser aged 41 and the oldest Webb and Walsh, both 65.

MacDonald at 58 was much the same age as was his contemporary Stanley Baldwin when he first took office (56 in 1923), but the trend has been towards youth since the 1960s. So, although MacDonald was younger than many of those who succeeded him (Chamberlain 68 in 1937, Churchill 66 in 1940, Attlee 62 in 1945, Macmillan 63 in 1957, Douglas-Home 60 in 1963, Callaghan 64 in 1976),[15] he was older than Wilson (48), Heath (54), Thatcher (54) and Major (47) and several 21st century Prime Ministers (Blair, Cameron, Truss and Sunak).[16]

There may be at least four factors at work here. Probably the most significant is the chance element in politics: Harold Macmillan being preferred to RA Butler as Eden's replacement to lead the Tories, or the premature deaths of Nye Bevan, Hugh Gaitskell, John Smith and Iain

---

[15] Eden was the same age as MacDonald, 58, when he eventually became Prime Minister in 1955.

[16] Three recent Prime Ministers were of comparable age: Gordon Brown (56 in 2007), Theresa May (60 in 2016) and Boris Johnson (55 in 2019).

Macleod - without which Wilson, Blair and Heath might never have become Prime Minister. In most instances youth won out. Another example is the Social Democratic Party (SDP) split from Labour that burned briefly but brightly between 1981 and the late 1980s, and removed both Roy Jenkins and David Owen from any future prospects in the Labour Party. Secondly, the trend towards youth exemplified by John F Kennedy's 1960 election as US President was mirrored elsewhere, including in the UK, and amplified by the professionalisation of politics where a few years of law (for example) might be followed by, or combined with, political ascent. Others went straight from university into think-tank or backroom jobs in politics. Thirdly, the Second World War may have reduced the political pool amongst a certain age and motivated a younger generation to get involved. The openings were there. The fourth and final factor concerned education or, more accurately, schooling in the case of these Labour MPs.

Education

Labour MPs in 1924 (including the Cabinet) had often left school before they were 15 (frequently some years earlier) and thus started their working lives, and often their political advancement, at an earlier age than their Tory counterparts. Indeed only Webb, Buxton, Trevelyan, Wedgwood and the law officers were still at school at 15.

No doubt there were both push and pull factors at work, the former being family pressure to add to the household income and the 'pull' ones being community (and family) examples and the desire to earn a wage. That several soon developed in Trade Union roles suggests that they had organisational talent, allied with representational abilities and speaking skills. Further formal schooling would not have provided them with any more and it certainly would not have ensured they earned respect and trust from their work colleagues.

Working-class backgrounds

The first twenty years of the 20th century saw major legislatives changes, with the 1911 Parliament Act having a profound impact on British politics. While the best known aspect may be the limitations imposed on the House of Lords power to delay Bills, particularly money Bills, agreed by the Commons, probably the most significant was the associated introduction of salaries for MPs.[17] This meant that parliamentary representation was no longer restricted to those whose wealth (inherited or otherwise) permitted it, but in theory opened it to all (as long as they were men; women would have to wait). This inevitably strengthened Labour Party representation and, while it did not precipitate the demise of the Liberal Party, it contributed to Labour becoming the main opposition to the Tories.[18]

However, eleven of the eighteen MPs in the Labour Cabinet had been in parliament before 1911 - though in two cases, they had sat as Liberals and personal and family financial resources were not an issue (Buxton and Trevelyan). The others were MacDonald, Clynes, Snowden, Henderson, JH

---

[17] Henry Pelling, 'The politics of the Osborne judgment', *Historical Journal*, 25 (1982), 889-909
The Osborne judgment in 1909 was against the automatic political levy by trade unions, a small part of which would be used to pay sponsored Labour MPs. The payment of MPs was brought in alongside the 1911 budget and the rest of the judgment reversed in 1913.

[18] Hugh Stephens, 'Party re-alignment in Britain, 1900-1925: A preliminary analysis', *Social Science History*, 6 (1982), 35-66

Thomas, Walsh, Adamson, Wedgwood and Jowett. Apart from the wealth of the Wedgwood family in which Josiah Wedgwood would have shared, all had an undeniably working-class background yet had sat in parliament before MPs were paid. How had they managed this?

In the 1912/13 session the Commons sat for 206 days but this was exceptional. Most sessions were much briefer. In the thirteen years before the First World War the average was 155 days per year, or about five months.[19] During the war itself, there was a reduction to 146 days and a further reduction to an average of 144 days in the five years 1919-1923 after it. During the 1924 Labour government the House sat for 129 days (across roughly nine months from February to October). So, even for the few who attended every sitting, being a parliamentary MP took up less than half the year, enabling many to continue their non-parliamentary work.

Clynes, Henderson, JH Thomas, Walsh, Adamson and Jowett had been sponsored by their Trade Unions, and it was likely that they were subsidised by these Unions.[20] Henderson was in addition on the Board of the *Newcastle Evening News*. In his analysis of English Cabinets 1801-1924, Harold Laski notes

> [t]he non-trade-union section of the Labour Party is ... in much the same position as members of other parties. They are lawyers, rentiers, teachers, doctors, and their ability to pursue a

---

[19] Number of sitting days in the House of Commons by session since 1900 - House of Commons Library (parliament.uk) - accessed 27 November 2023

[20] Chris Wrigley, 'At the crossroads: The Labour Party, the trade unions and the choices for the democratic left' in Lucy Bland and Richard Carr (eds), *Labour, British Radicalism and the First World War* (Manchester, 2018)

parliamentary career depends upon the same considerations as affect the Conservative or the Liberal. The number of professions compatible with a political career is limited; and, broadly, the trade union official in the Labour Party has the same kind of advantage as the rentier or the lawyer.[21]

MacDonald and Snowden had other arrangements.

In 1896 MacDonald had married Margaret Gladstone whose private income was sufficient for them to live in 'a roomy chaotic flat' in Lincoln's Inn Fields. It must have been roomy indeed for they had six children and although Margaret died in 1911, five years into MacDonald's career as MP for Leicester West, his financial circumstances were unchanged. Indeed his wife's trust fund had increased since their marriage and he continued to benefit from it.[22] In addition, MPs were about to be salaried and MacDonald had succeeded George Barnes in 1911 as Leader of the Labour Party. Although MacDonald had been Secretary of the Labour Representation Committee since 1900, this did not increase his finances; rather he was expected to fund the role himself and provide the London office. What this role did ensure was that MacDonald was one of the successful LRC candidates when the Liberals stood aside in thirty seats in 1906.[23]

Snowden's background and ill-health had tempered his expectations and ensured his financial circumstances remained modest. He was in the

---

[21] Harold Laski, 'The personnel of the English Cabinet, 1801-1924', *American Political Science Review*, 22 (1928), 12-31

[22] MacDonald's Oxford Dictionary of National Biography entry

[23] See Labour Representation Committee in Oxford Dictionary of National Biography themes.

ILP from 1893 and candidate for Keighley in 1895. Editor of the *Keighley Journal* from 1898, he stood in the 1900 election for the LRC at Blackburn and then in 1902 at Warrington. Unsuccessful in both contests, he earned a living as a speaker and jobbing commentator from 1902 before becoming MP for Blackburn in 1906, again on the Labour (LRC) ticket. He and Ethel Annakin, a schoolteacher, married in 1905 and after their marriage both earned their living through journalism, books and pamphlets (often suffrage ones in her case). Snowden was out of parliament from 1918 until 1922 when he was returned for Colne Valley. Despite representing two Lancashire constituencies for 23 years, Snowden reverted to his Yorkshire roots when he was ennobled in 1931 as Viscount Snowden of Ickornshaw and is claimed by Yorkshire as well.[24]

LANCASHIRE POLITICS IN THE 1920s

The early 1920s were turbulent, particularly in Liverpool 'which saw the worst of the violence' that unemployment provoked.[25] There were police strikes as well, and while Labour's profile increased as a result of the unrest and the anxiety it aroused, if they formed the next government they would be expected to reduce unemployment and dampen the unrest.

Baldwin called the 1923 election over the imposition of tariffs on (non-food) imports. In his view this was the only solution to high levels of unemployment and would encourage other countries to dismantle their

---

[24] For example, "Our Philip": The Early Career of Philip Snowden (bradfordhistorical.org.uk) - accessed 29 November 2023
[25] Charlotte Wildman, 'Urban transformation in Liverpool and Manchester, 1918-1939', *Historical Journal*, 55 (2012), 119-143

barriers, opening up a wider range of markets to British exports. It was a matter of principle because Baldwin's predecessor Bonar Law had promised not to re-introduce such tariffs.

Labour and the Liberals were strongly opposed to protectionism, for both parties fundamentally believed in free trade - as did Lancashire generally since the cotton industry and the shipping interests depended on it. One difficulty was that many of the seats in Liverpool had a long tradition of returning Conservatives. This point has been underlined by Jeffery (citing two other authors):

> The modern Labour Party in Liverpool came into existence in 1917, and began its first year of normal activity in 1918. However, beginning with its birth as the ILP, Merseyside proved 'to be an extremely weak area for the party'.[26]

Liverpool Edge Hill was the only one of the eleven Liverpool seats to switch to Labour in 1923, the Party's first toe-hold in the city. Seven seats remained Conservative, two were won by the Liberals[27] and TP O'Connor, the Irish Nationalist, continued to represent the Liverpool Scotland constituency (as he had since 1885).

Prior to the election the picture in Manchester was more mixed, with six of the ten seats held by Conservatives and four by Labour. Five of the Conservative constituencies (Manchester Blackley, Exchange, Moss Side, Rusholme and Withington) all fell to the Liberals, with the Conservatives

---

[26] David Jeffery, *Whatever Happened to Tory Liverpool? Success, decline and irrelevance since 1945* (Liverpool, 2023), 43
[27] Hugh Rathbone in Liverpool Wavertree, Sydney Jones in Liverpool West Derby

only retaining Manchester Hulme. Labour retained the four seats it already held (Ardwick, Clayton, Gorton and JR Clynes in Manchester Platting). For one historian of the Conservative Party the implications were dire:

> Manchester Exchange, a Conservative seat, was the first to be declared. It was lost to the Liberals on an 11.8% swing. It was the harbinger of Tory disaster in Lancashire, a bastion of the party since Disraeli's day, and elsewhere in the north-west with its deep attachment to free trade in the interests of the cotton industry. The Liberals won five of the ten Manchester seats, their first victories in the city since 1910.[28]

In the rest of Lancashire fifteen seats changed hands. As the Table below shows, the Tories were the largest party in Lancashire with 22 seats prior to the election, but lost half of them, gaining only one (Middleton and Prestwich from the Liberals). The Liberals almost doubled their representation (going from nine seats before to 16 after), but it was Labour who became the largest party with 19 (nearly 40%) of the 48 Lancashire seats. These 19 seats accounted for one in ten of the Labour MPs elected.

The seven seats the Tories lost to the Liberals were Blackpool, Darwen, Lancaster, Lonsdale, Royton, Southport and Stalybridge & Hyde. The four Labour gained were Rotherham, Salford South, Salford West and Warrington. (In addition, Labour lost Accrington

---

[28] How Stanley Baldwin lost the premiership a few months after achieving it, 100 years ago | Lord Lexden OBE (alistairlexden.org.uk) - accessed 29 November 2023

and Rochdale to the Liberals, but gained one of the two seats in Bolton from them.)[29]

	Lancashire Constituencies				
Party	Total before GE	Seats held	Seats gained	Seats lost	Total after GE
Conservative and Unionist	22	11	1	11	12
Labour	16	14	5	2	19
Liberal	9	7	9	2	16
Other (Independent)	1	1			1

Table: Lancashire constituency results in 1923 General Election

As one American academic described the results at the time:

> Unquestionably the most important single factor in deciding the election was the misery ... of a large section of society, which voiced its discontent against hunger and unemployment by

---

[29] The seats held were:
Liberals - one of two Blackburn seats, Bootle, Heywood and Radcliffe, one of two Oldham seats, one of two Preston seats, one of two Stockport seats, Stretford
Labour - Burnley, Colne Valley, Eccles, Farnworth, Ince, Leigh, Nelson and Colne, Newton, one of two Oldham seats, one of two Preston seats, St Helens, Salford North, Westhoughton, Wigan
Tories - one of two Blackburn seats, one of two Bolton seats, Bury, Chorley, Clitheroe, Fylde, Ormskirk, Rossendale, one of two Stockport seats, Waterloo, Widnes
Independent - Mossley

voting for Labour, because it promised them more than either of the older parties. Twelve months of "tranquillity" had increased the sullenness of the working classes, because it had not decreased unemployment or materially bettered housing conditions. The same government, moreover, had economised at the expense of their children's future ... [30]

This was especially the case in the north-west, with the prominent industries of the region among those most badly affected in the country. For example, production in the cotton industry peaked in 1920, rapidly declining thereafter, not least as one of the largest export markets in India developed its own technology.[31] Indeed, with the exception of Northern Ireland, the north-west region had the highest level of unemployment in 1923. At 14.5% one person in seven was out of work in the region. This compared with one in sixteen in Wales, which then had the lowest rate (though it would rapidly increase), and one in ten in the south-east, London, south-west and midlands (between 9.2% and 10.7%). Although the north-east would soon become the area with the most

---

[30] William T Morgan, 'The British elections of December 1923', *American Political Science Review,* 18 (1924), 331-340

[31] Andy Phelps et al, *The Textile Mills of Lancashire: The Legacy* (Lancaster, undated). Available at https://historicengland.org.uk/images-books/publications/textile-mills-lancashire-legacy/textile-mills-lancashire-legacy/ - accessed 30 November 2023
Also GW Daniels and J Jewkes, 'The post-war depression in the Lancashire cotton industry', *Journal of the Royal Statistical Society*, 91 (1928), 153-206 provides a sub-regional analysis showing the rise of competitors in Japan and Egypt and the impact in particular Lancashire mill towns.

unemployed in England (peaking at nearly one in three in 1932), the rate there was 12.2% in 1923.[32]

LANCASHIRE MPs IN THE CABINET

Arthur Henderson was the first to be elected in 1903, though this was for Barnard Castle in County Durham rather than a Lancashire seat. He was MP there until 1918, and would subsequently represent four constituencies with only the Burnley berth lasting longer than a few years. This nomadic career affected the seniority that he otherwise enjoyed among his party colleagues. In 1906 Snowden was elected for Blackburn, Clynes for Manchester North East and Walsh for Ince. Only Walsh (and Shaw more briefly 1918-1931) would continue to represent the same constituency without a break throughout their parliamentary career (1906-1929).[33] Indeed he might have continued to do so had he not died that year aged 70.

Of the five, it is Walsh and Shaw who are least well-known and on whom this section concentrates.

Stephen Walsh

Born in Liverpool and orphaned as an infant, Walsh started in the pits near Wigan aged 13 (initially as a pony boy).[34] Clark states, and his DNB entry implies, that Walsh was active in trade union affairs from an early

---

[32] Meredith Paker, 'Industrial, regional and gender divides in British unemployment between the wars' (2020), 10, 51. Available at jobmarketpaper-meredithpakerpdf (ox.ac.uk) - accessed 30 November 2023

[33] Clynes represented Manchester North East (Platting) for longer but was out of parliament for four years in the 1930s.

[34] Clark, Men of 1924, 159

age. However, it was when aged 31 in 1890 that he first took a formal position, district officer and secretary of his local union. Shortly afterwards he was elected a councillor for Ashton in Makerfield, one of the Urban District Councils (UDCs) that came into being in 1894. According to Yvonne Eckersley,

> From the outset Ashton councillors, mainly mine owners, managers, colliery officials and large factory owners, were obstructive. At the council's inaugural meeting their hostility was particularly marked. Acting out of step with nearby councils, they rejected Stephen Walsh's request that meetings begin at the end of the working day, voting instead for mid-afternoon.[35]

Walsh was to draw on his UDC knowledge in a parliamentary speech in 1910, contrasting the benefits accruing to landowners while those who improved and developed land paid higher rates:

> I can give as a case in point the council on which I sat as a member shortly after the year 1894. A railway runs through that little township about six miles in length. ... The improvements brought about by this railway were very great, but the landowners in that particular area received all the benefit, while the railway, which had really been a great boon to the district

---

[35] Yvonne Eckersley, 'Out of the pits and into parliament: Part 2, Winning hearts, minds and votes', *Past Forward*, 85 (2020), 4-6

and a still greater boon to the landowners, was burdened with taxation and assessed at the rate of £15,000 a year.[36]

His next union position was as miner's agent in the Lancashire and Cheshire Miners' Federation in 1901. At that stage the Lancashire and Cheshire Federation remained outside the national Miners Federation of Great Britain formed in 1890, preferring autonomy to power and influence, despite the 1893 lock-out demonstrating vividly the strength of the larger group. Perhaps because the local Federation was less able to counter the mine-owners, it turned towards parliament as the solution to their grievances.[37] In the Wigan area miners 'constitute[d] the majority of the electorate' which, with the exception of Leigh, was not the position elsewhere in Lancashire. However, the Lancashire coalfield 'had many pitmen who were Tories' and there were no guaranteed union seats - even in Wigan.[38] Nearby Ince had elected Sam Woods as Lib-Lab MP as early as 1892 but he proved himself too close to the Liberals and less willing to seek reforms than his electorate expected.[39] His anti-socialism drew criticism from Keir Hardie and Beatrice Webb and in 1895 he was defeated by the Conservative coal-owner Colonel Blundell. In 1906 the sitting Tory Blundell was opposed by Walsh, who was fortunate that no

---

[36] Parliamentary Debates (Commons), 17, 27 April 1910, 547

[37] These included regulations that would reduce the relatively high levels of death and injury, an eight hour day as in other coalfields, employers remaining liable for industrial injury rather than miners being forced to contract out, and the appointment of checkweighmen. Raymond Challinor, *The Lancashire and Cheshire Miners* (Newcastle upon Tyne, 1972), 213-214

[38] Challinor, Miners, 214-215

[39] The decision to contest Ince had been taken by the miners in 1890 and Walsh was secretary of the local parliamentary committee that created an election fund. Challinor, Miners, 221

Liberal stood to split the anti-Tory vote and that the election took place during a miners' strike, reducing the likelihood of votes for Blundell. In the event Walsh's majority was over 4,600 or 40% of those who voted.[40]

The Labour Party generally supported the country's declaration of war in 1914, but several prominent ILP MPs were against it (including MacDonald, Snowden and Jowett).

> In April 1915, ... the Socialist National Defence Committee [was formed] ... to counter the Socialist opponents of the war. This vociferously chauvinistic body included Dan Irving of the BSP [British Socialist Party], Joseph Burgess of the ILP, Stewart Headlam of the Fabian Society, HG Wells, Robert Blatchford, and some Labour members of Parliament like John Hodge, CH Roberts and Stephen Walsh. A year later it became the British Workers National League, dedicated to peace by victory ...[41]

In the first full year of WWI, Walsh confined his Commons speeches to coal mining and pit accidents, with one exception on the question of whether National Service should be made compulsory. This enabled him to demonstrate his patriotism (as well as that of his fellow workers) and illustrates why Walsh would be the obvious (perhaps only) choice as Secretary for War in the 1924 government.

---

[40] Challinor, Miners, 233-234
[41] Ralph Miliband, *Parliamentary Socialism: A Study in the Politics of Labour* (Pontypool, 1972 [orig. 1961]), 44

I represent, and have done for thirty-six years, what I think is the greatest labour organisation in the Kingdom. We undertook - 800,000 of us - that during the continuance of the War not a single labour dispute should take place. ...

Eighty per cent. of the Members of this House came in as the supporters of the voluntary system, and I do not think that 20 per cent. came in, in 1910, as supporters of compulsion. Before we change the system upon which the liberties and prosperity of the nation have been built up we must be fairly satisfied that the necessities of the situation require it. ... I believe, and I think the vast majority of the nation agrees, that the welfare of the State is the highest law. If it is necessary for the preservation of the State, and of all those liberties and ideals with which the State is associated, to revert to Conscription, then Conscription it must be. But the evidence must be unmistakable and unassailable.

I never did trust a Tory in many things. The only one thing in which I thought he was equally good with myself was in the love of country. I believe Tories to be wrong in almost every particular except that, but I have always given them credit for honest loyalty. I believe they desire to do their best according to their light for the good of their country.[42]

Walsh's Financial Secretary at the War Office was the Durham miner Jack Lawson and his Under-Secretary the public school educated but

---

[42] Parliamentary Debates (Commons), 74, 15 September 1915, 116-117

thoroughly socialist Clement Attlee.[43] Elected as MPs in 1919 and 1922 respectively, they forged a lifelong friendship with Lawson Secretary of State for War in Attlee's 1945 government.

Tom Shaw

Shaw complemented Walsh by representing that other great body of Lancashire workers, the weavers. Like Walsh he had a trade union background, first as secretary of the Colne Weavers Association, then as the first secretary of the Northern Counties Textile Federation and subsequently from 1911 secretary of the International Federation of Textile Workers - a post he held until his death in 1938 with only a two year gap during the 1929-1931 Labour government.

Like Walsh he supported the First World War, in Shaw's case as director of national service for the west midlands region. He opposed a call for industrial strikes internationally to prevent war (i.e., to promote worker solidarity in several countries against aggressive imperialism that depended on workers killing each other). When a motion to this effect was considered by the 1912 Labour Party conference, Shaw spoke against it:

> War between country and country is a bad thing, but in case of such a war any attempt of a General Strike to prevent the people defending their country would result in civil war which was ten times worse than war between nation and nation.[44]

---

[43] Jack Lawson, *A Man's Life* (London, 1944), 168
[44] Miliband, Socialism, 41

Shaw went further in later years, asking the 1919 Labour Party conference to declare 'against the principle of industrial action in purely political matters'.[45]

One question is why MacDonald chose Shaw as Minister of Labour ahead of others with a trade union background. Shaw's unionism remained active and international. He had proved an effective Labour whip in the 1918-1922 period, not least because his speeches repeatedly showed him to be imbued with Labour values, thereby earning the respect of colleagues: for example, he advocated free trade because he abhorred the impact of protectionism on the poorest;[46] he argued that collectivism was superior to individualist approaches and had contributed significantly to winning WWI;[47] he recognised the scourge of underemployment that, like unemployment, damaged a family budget and took its toll on health and welfare;[48] and he promoted the equal treatment of women.[49] He railed against unequal treatment for the working classes and the hypocrisy that Tories such as Edward Carson were treated with leniency and bias:

> Let me point out what the right hon. and learned Member for Belfast said ... He claimed that he had an army at his command, an Ulster volunteer army which he could call out if this Parliament passed a law to which he objected. That was the essence of his claim with regard to the army. He claimed also

---

[45] Miliband, Socialism, 74
[46] Parliamentary Debates (Commons), 114, 25 March 1919, 342-347
[47] Parliamentary Debates (Commons), 115, 16 May 1919, 1956-1958
[48] Parliamentary Debates (Commons), 125, 25 February 1920, 1855
[49] Parliamentary Debates (Commons), 125, 27 February 1920, 2085-2087

that he had a government which he would call together if Parliament decided against the policy that he advocated. I thought the name of His Majesty the King was "George". It appears, however, that in a certain part of Ireland his majesty is "Edward". That citizens of this realm can be permitted to have an army and a government and yet not break the law seems to me very strange. If we tell our people that there is no breach of the law in claiming an army and a government of their own to use against this Government if Parliament passes a law of which they do not approve, what will they reply? Some of us are fighting day after day to prevent breaches of the law; we are fighting day after day to convince working men who do not believe there is equality before the law that the safest course is constitutional action and constitutional methods. And yet here we have men who can go on platforms and say things that we know would land working men into gaol inside of a week from the utterance of them. How can we conscientiously go to our people and say the people are equal before the law, when we know in our heart of hearts that they are not equal?[50]

After the War trade disputes no longer automatically triggered an accusation of unpatriotic behaviour, but they were still portrayed as against the national interest. In early 1924 an Emergency Committee was convened to deal with the docks and London transport strikes called by the TGWU. The Committee was chaired by Henderson with JH Thomas,

---

[50] Parliamentary Debates (Commons), 118, 16 July 1919, 516-518
Carson had given his speech four days earlier.

Viscount Chelmsford and Walsh the other members. They revived the Cabinet-level Supply and Transport Committee that Lloyd George had used to break strikes (such as the railway one in 1919). This left Shaw free to negotiate directly with both sides, which he did over the course of a week. Although the employers first agreed to a wage increase of 1 shilling a day from early March (half what the dockers were seeking), no settlement was reached. Shaw then appointed a Court of Inquiry under the Industrial Courts Act to look into the details on both sides.[51] The docks strike was then settled when the employers agreed to implement the rest of the workers' wage demand from May.[52] The subsequent tramway dispute required the Emergency Powers Act to be invoked on 28 March.[53] Three days later it was over.

> The Labour government [had come] down hard on the side of the public interest in order to prove their capacity to rule responsibly in the interest of all.[54]

JR Clynes, Arthur Henderson and Philip Snowden
These other three Cabinet MPs representing Lancashire constituencies had a higher profile in the contemporary parliamentary party and have

---

[51] Parliamentary Debates (Commons), 169, 18 February 1924, 1316-1318
[52] 22 Feb 1924 - DOCK STRIKE ENDED. - Trove (nla.gov.au) - accessed 17 January 2024
[53] The Privy Council met at Knowsley Hall, the home of the Earl of Derby, where the King was staying. Miliband, Socialism, 110 comments 'There was surely something very symbolic about the Proclamation being signed in the residence of a former Conservative Minister, who was also one of the richest men in England'.
[54] Ralph H Desmarais, 'Strikebreaking and the Labour government of 1924', *Journal of Contemporary History*, 8 (1973), 165-175

remained better known subsequently. By 1924, even though Henderson was initially out of parliament and Snowden relatively recently returned, they were firmly established as Labour grandees. Indeed, Clynes and Snowden had joined the ILP when it was first formed in 1893, a year earlier than MacDonald.

Snowden had concentrated on financial policy since becoming an MP in 1906. He was chairman of the national ILP council during his years out of parliament and also used the time to write one of his most enduring books, *Labour and National Finance* (1920).[55] This, along with his financial expertise and speeches in parliament, confirmed that he would be the natural choice as Chancellor of the Exchequer if Labour formed a government.

Henderson had succeeded Keir Hardie as party chairman (effectively leader) from 1908 to 1910. He had been in Asquith's war cabinet as the one Labour member since May 1915 and initially remained in Lloyd George's from December 1916 until he resigned in fury the following August. This resignation increased his credibility in Labour ranks, enhanced further when he reorganised the party organisation to permit individual membership (as well as through affiliated trade unions and other organisations). The 1918 Labour Party conference approved a new policy statement that he had been instrumental in drawing up and, with Sidney Webb, he led on formulating the party's proposals on unemployment in the early 1920s. Although Henderson might have preferred to be Foreign Secretary in the 1924 government, MacDonald

---

[55] Snowden Oxford Dictionary of National Biography entry

combined this role with that of Prime Minister, and out of parliament Henderson had to accept the consolation prize of Home Secretary.

JR Clynes had opposed Labour involvement in the Asquith coalition government but served himself in the subsequent Lloyd George one. He had been Labour party chairman (i.e., leader) in 1921 but was defeated by MacDonald after the 1922 election. As vice-chairman he moved the vote of no confidence against Baldwin's government in January 1924 and in the subsequent Labour government was Lord Privy Seal and in effect Leader in the Commons (though technically MacDonald's Deputy Leader there). Throughout the government's tenure, for example, it was Clynes who laid out the following week's business in the Commons.[56] This was not one of the three great offices of state, as were those held by Snowden, Henderson and MacDonald himself as Foreign Secretary, but it was far from insignificant and enabled Clynes to retain his prominence in parliament, speaking frequently and at length.[57] Clynes was never formally Deputy Prime Minister but according to Clark it was he that lived at 11 Downing Street rather than Snowden.[58] On Clynes' death in 1949 aged 80 it was Attlee, by then Prime Minister, who led the parliamentary tributes.

---

[56] Mr John Clynes: speeches in 1924 (Hansard) (parliament.uk) - accessed 31 January 2024
There was no Deputy Prime Minister as such.
[57] Leader of the Commons was a more substantial post when the Prime Minister was in the House of Lords. Prime Ministers who sat in the Commons generally retained the role themselves (though Lloyd George relinquished it in favour of Bonar Law in 1916).
[58] Clark, Men of 1924, 123

THE 1924 LABOUR GOVERNMENT IN OFFICE

Achievements

Inexperienced and inheriting severe social difficulties, MacDonald's government benefited from novelty, substantial goodwill in the community and the absence of any prior commitments in the Commons to hinder them. However, expectations were high, probably unrealistically so, and Baldwin's preference, even enthusiasm, for Labour to replace the Tories in power, rather than the Liberals, was not because he thought they could succeed but because he was certain they would fail.[59] As I have put it elsewhere,

> This was both a matter of principle and deft tactics ... An inexperienced Labour government at this time would certainly be more cautious and have to weigh more carefully the gap between attractive-sounding promises and costed initiatives against which their delivery could be tested. On both counts they would be weaker, making them less of a threat to the constitution or Conservative recovery. On the other hand an administration led by the Liberals might enable that party to re-group or Labour to develop their experience without bearing full accountability and to promote themselves more positively to the electorate next time. Baldwin's view was that a Labour administration would be in the Conservative party's interests, a

---

[59] Stuart Ball, *Portrait of a Party: The Conservative Party in Britain 1918-1945* (Oxford, 2013), 72 confirms this.

happy conjunction of strategy and principle, but a high-risk gamble nonetheless.[60]

Neville Chamberlain was also of the view that a Labour government 'would be too weak to do much harm but not too weak to get discredited'.[61] The risk for Labour was that they would try to do too much too soon.

In the event MacDonald's Cabinet proved to be moderate and restrained, in line with the strategy of 'gradualness' that the Fabian Sidney Webb had espoused and with the policy of moderation MacDonald had advocated ahead of the election to demonstrate Labour's fitness for office.[62] As the Labour backbencher Haden Guest was to write subsequently, the 1924 government showed itself British first, purely theoretical (i.e., Socialist) second and, apart from the Ministry of Health agreement over housing, had a disappointing record overall. Later observers concurred about Wheatley's Housing Act: their 'only lasting legislative success'.[63] Seldon describes MacDonald's years as Prime Minister as 'a negative legacy'.[64] Haden Guest concluded like Cowling that the Labour government had flunked the real question of 'evolution or

---

[60] Hugh Gault, *Making the Heavens Hum: Kingsley Wood and the Art of the Possible 1881-1924* (Cambridge, 2014), 215
[61] Keith Feiling, *The Life of Neville Chamberlain* (London, 1946), 111
[62] Miliband, Socialism, 97
[63] Miliband, Socialism, 108 adds that it 'paved the way for a substantial increase over the following years in municipal house building'. He also identifies a handful of other 'very modest improvements'.
[64] Anthony Seldon, *The Impossible Office? The History of the British Prime Minister* (Cambridge, 2021), 122
This includes Seldon's assessment of MacDonald's later years as Prime Minister from 1929.

revolution' so as not to frighten the horses (the bourgeoisie through a capital levy and those who feared nationalisation of the means of production).[65] Dilks provides another perspective on their conscientious, but deliberately unadventurous, approach:

> [The Cabinet was] considerably more businesslike than those of Lloyd George, Bonar Law or Baldwin. The Ministers read their papers. If the agenda had not been completed, they would re-assemble the same afternoon or the next day.[66]

This is faint praise and the government had no long-term impact on unemployment, their biggest challenge. Levels reduced slightly in 1925 but rose thereafter and continued to do so into the 1930s.

Difficulties

On 12 February MacDonald had set out the Government's intentions. As interesting as the wide range of policies he put forward, was his opening statement that the Commons would have to change its habits now that the largest party was no longer in power. Labour, he asserted, would not be turned out by Members rushing in to vote in the hope of catching the Government napping:

---

[65] L Haden Guest, *Where is Labour Going? A Political Pamphlet* (London, 1927), 69
[66] David Dilks, *Neville Chamberlain - Vol. 1: Pioneering and Reform, 1896-1929* (Cambridge, 1984), 368

I am going out on no such issue … The Labour Government will [only] go out if it be defeated upon substantial issues, issues of principle, issues that really matter. It will go out if the responsible leaders of either party or any party move a direct vote of no confidence, and carry that vote.[67]

Inevitably the Conservative opposition thought this too good an opportunity to miss, lodging a vote of no confidence in the government soon after. In late March Henderson was challenged about whether certain items of Communist party correspondence were still being stopped in the post or whether the Home Secretary had deferred to his party's representations by relaxing previous precautions. Henderson, refusing to be caught out, declined to say, arguing that to do so would be against the public interest.[68] The following day the Conservatives proposed that £100 should be stopped from Clynes' salary as Lord Privy Seal over the inadequate way he had handled the Rent Restrictions Bill in Parliament.[69]

In 1924 the book 'Constructive Conservativism' challenged the Conservatives to look to the future, rather than being content just to police or caretake the past, for 'It is in action that principles come into play'.[70] The author Noel Skelton's analysis was reminiscent of Disraeli's 1832 statement that he was 'a Conservative to preserve all that is good in our Constitution, a Radical to remove all that is bad'. It was a call to action

---

[67] Parliamentary Debates (Commons), 169, 12 February 1924, 749-750
[68] Parliamentary Debates (Commons), 171, 20 March 1924, 617-618
[69] Parliamentary Debates (Commons), 171, 21 March 1924, 837ff
[70] Noel Skelton, *Constructive Conservatism* (London, 1924)

and acted as a goad to Baldwin and as a pick-me-up for a party in the doldrums.

Demise

In September the Conservatives began to attack the government's achilles, their links with Russia and their intention to agree a treaty with them. Baldwin and his front-bench colleagues might have been content to embarrass the Government over their Russian overtures and then over the *Workers' Weekly* case. Kingsley Wood, however, went further, attacking MacDonald over the proposed treaty with Russia and over his character and motivation, noting that the government would not easily go out of office unless pushed out and describing the Prime Minister as the 'modern political Artful Dodger'. Wood claimed to fear public reaction to the Russian treaty and hoped that Baldwin would move a vote of censure when Parliament returned in October. Furthermore, the country should not be providing a loan to Russia at that moment when any spare money was needed to reduce unemployment at home.[71]

Later that month Wood revived the question of seditious articles that had been published in *Workers' Weekly*.[72] The essence was that the *Workers' Weekly* offices were raided at the start of August, Hastings confirmed in Parliament the following day that charges would be pressed and the parliamentary recess started on the next. When the charges were

---

[71] *Yorkshire Observer*, 24 September 1924

[72] The case is described at length in many places: for example, from the perspective of Thomas Jones, deputy Cabinet secretary for four Prime Ministers, and from the point of view of the Labour Attorney-General, as well as in many biographies and in more general works. For example, John Shepherd and Keith Laybourn, *Britain's First Labour Government* (Basingstoke, 2006), 168ff

then withdrawn within the week, it seemed that the heat had gone out of the issue and there was certainly no indication that 'Within a few days this seemingly not very important matter [would] burst into a conflagration'.[73]

When Parliament resumed at the end of September, the Attorney-General was asked to explain why the prosecution had been withdrawn. When Hastings argued that a jury would be unlikely to convict the *Workers' Weekly* editor and a prosecution would therefore be inappropriate, he was asked why in that case the prosecuting counsel had stated that it had been withdrawn because of representations.[74] Hastings was unable to clarify the matter. The Prime Minister was then asked whether he had given any directions to the Director of Public Prosecutions to withdraw the prosecution.[75] MacDonald denied even having been consulted, a reply that several of his colleagues, and some senior officials, knew to be incorrect.

Wood returned to the attack on 2 October when he put a written question to the Attorney-General asking for a copy of the information given to counsel in the *Workers' Weekly* proceedings. Hastings refused, describing it as an unprecedented request.[76] Provocatively, Wood had asked a little earlier about MacDonald's salary and 'whether he had found the emoluments … insufficient, and has had to go to a private citizen …'. There was uproar, with Labour MPs interrupting with cries of "Dirty" and asking the Speaker to name Wood for this insult. As the *Liverpool Post*

---

[73] Patrick Hastings, *The Autobiography of Patrick Hastings* (London, 1948), 239
[74] Parliamentary Debates (Commons), 177, 30 September 1924, 8-11
[75] Parliamentary Debates (Commons), 177, 30 September 1924, 16
[76] Parliamentary Debates (Commons), 177, 2 October 1924, 360

reported, the Speaker stopped the question and rebuked Wood for putting it.[77] Some Conservatives also disapproved of this un-parliamentary and un-gentlemanly behaviour and the *Liverpool Post* observed that Wood 'carries partisanship to an extreme point'.[78] But Wood had also made the allegation outside Parliament a week earlier, a step he would not have risked if there was the slightest doubt about the underlying truth.[79] Wood pointed out, damagingly for any Labour politician, but particularly for the Prime Minister, that MacDonald was a shareholder in a 'profitable trading concern' (McVitie's) to the extent of £30,000, shares given to him by the owner 'for the purpose …of running a motor car', his Daimler. MacDonald had been open about this, or rather he had been naïve given the way that opponents could portray it.

On 8 October MacDonald made a statement correcting his earlier reply on 30 September, but still failing to respond fully, thereby deepening the hole he was in even further. The Labour MP for Dartford asked him not to say any more.[80] Later that sitting the formal debate censuring the Government for its handling of the *Workers' Weekly* prosecution began. The Government lost the censure vote 364 votes to 159 and, rather than submit to the proposed Select Committee to examine the withdrawal of the prosecution, resigned.[81]

Parliament was prorogued the following day and the next general election campaign began. Labour's electoral prospects were further

---

[77] Parliamentary Debates (Commons), 177, 2 October 1924, 316-317
[78] *Liverpool Post*, 3 October 1924
[79] In a speech at Woolwich Masonic Hall in the interval of a Conservative Association concert - reported in *Kentish Mercury*, 26 September 1924.
[80] Parliamentary Debates (Commons), 177, 8 October 1924, 512-517
[81] Parliamentary Debates (Commons), 177, 8 October 1924, 581-704

damaged during the campaign itself when the Zinoviev letter emerged. This purported to be from the President of the Third International Grigori Zinoviev promoting the supposed Communist aspirations of army sedition and worker uprising. The letter was published on 24 October, though the Foreign Office had received it a fortnight earlier and one of the accusations was that MacDonald, sent it because of his responsibility for foreign affairs, had suppressed it in his role as Labour Party leader. The day after publication senior Tories attacked it in a 'well-briefed chorus'.[82] A copy had been sent independently to the *Daily Mail* as well and the paper ruthlessly exploited the Labour Party implications, a credible link given the proposed treaty with Russia the Labour government had pursued.[83] Although Zinoviev disclaimed responsibility two days before the general election, he was not believed and Labour scepticism about the letter was easily discounted as predictable. The facts were buried in the web of political intrigue.[84]

The Conservatives were returned as the largest party with 413 seats out of 615, a net gain of 155, while Labour had a net loss of 40 seats and the Liberals were reduced to 40. Sixteen million people had voted, 80% of the electorate, an increase from 14.5m (74%) in 1923. The Tories' vote increased by 2m to 7.4m and Labour's by over a million to 5.5m. The

---

[82] Lewis Chester, Stephen Fay and Hugo Young, *The Zinoviev Letter* (London, 1967), 12
Also Gabriel Gorodetsky, *The Precarious Truce: Anglo-Soviet Relations 1924-1927* (Cambridge, 1977), 35-52, 54-56
[83] Parliamentary Debates (Commons), 215, 19 March 1928, 52
The treaty was never ratified.
[84] Ball, Conservative Party, 91: 'A case of exploiting a golden opportunity rather than a planned attack'.

Liberal vote reduced by more than 1.25m, leaving Labour as the clear party of opposition to the Conservatives for the foreseeable future.

PARALLELS WITH TODAY

There are of course contrasts with today, some of which were pointed out in the Introduction. But equally noticeable are the parallels.

In opposition it must look as though being in government is the only game in town. However, once in office it is quickly apparent that this does not automatically confer the means to bring about change. 'In office but not in power' is a phrase with which all governments thought impotent or ineffective are tarred. However, it applies to every government to a greater or lesser extent, especially when the delivery arms of government (the civil service, local government and the public sector generally) have been deskilled, devalued and denied the resources to develop in line with demands.

Then there are extraneous events that throw governments off course, constrain their room for manoeuvre or hijack their agenda. In recent years the Covid pandemic, conflicts in Ukraine, Sudan and the middle east have sucked all the attention from previous plans and objectives. Before that were Brexit and the international financial crisis, neither of which were anticipated or, many would argue, inevitable. Personal aggrandisement and institutional greed took centre stage to the detriment of many people less prominent or well-connected.

No wonder the key planetary challenge of climate crisis is dealt with so haphazardly and inconclusively. Why and how might government find the time to focus on this longer term threat when there are so many others more immediate? They would certainly not be forgiven if the immediate ones were not tackled. Consequently, dealing with the climate emergency can be deferred, even as the threat grows, and treated as somebody else's problem, often another country's and certainly another government's. Blaming it on someone else is always easier than confronting your own responsibility.

The same is true of geopolitics. Shaming and blaming the developing world or another out-group whose values are different from the west's, and therefore considered threatening because not understood, is a useful displacement and distraction from domestic problems, whereas co-operation would require more effort, foresight and diplomacy than has been evident recently. This used to be called leadership or statesmanship, but this is noticeably absent at present. Narrow political advantage trumps any substantive or lasting impact.

Action is constrained by legacy aspirations and public opinion, however mediated (press, polls or direct action, for example), as well as by events.

Finally, free speech brings with it the risk (or opportunity) of offending somebody else. The 1924 Labour government carefully formulated its pronouncements so as not to antagonise their opponents in the wider establishment as well as in parliament. But, as MacDonald discovered, there is only so much hedging your bets and prevarication that is permissible. Beyond that point it becomes dishonesty.

Appendix: Eighteen MPs in 1924 Labour Cabinet

Name	Post	Constituency (& dates)	Previous constituencies (& dates)	Previous parties (& dates)	Previous Cabinet posts (& dates)	Job(s) prior to politics	Parents; siblings	Place of birth	Age in 1924
Ramsay MacDonald (1866-1937)	PM & Foreign Secretary	Aberavon 1922-1929; later Seaham Harbour 1929-1935; Scottish Universities 1936-1937	Leicester (West) 1906-1918;	Social Democratic Federation 1885; Socialist Union later 1885; ILP 1894; LRC Sec 1900	None	farmworker; pupil teacher at 15; unemployed; invoice clerk at 20; private secretary to Liberal at 22	f ploughman, m farm servant; 0 b&s	Lossiemouth	58
JR Clynes (1869-1949)	Lord Privy Seal & Deputy Leader in Commons	Manchester NE (Platting) 1906-1931, 1935-1945	None	ILP 1893	None	mill half-timer at 10, full-timer at 12; TU organiser at 22	Irish f farmworker evicted 1851; 1b/5s	Oldham, Lancs.	55
Philip Snowden (1864-1937)	Chancellor of Exchequer	Colne Valley 1922-1931 then Lords	Blackburn 1906-1918	ILP 1893	None	insurance clerk at 15; civil servant at 22; paralysed at 27	weaver m & f moved to Nelson 1879; 0b/2s	Middleton Ickornshaw nr. Cowling, Yorks.	60
JH Thomas (1874-1949)	Colonial Secretary	Derby 1910-1936	None	Swindon Council 1901-?	None	p-t shop errand boy at 9; shops and decorating from 12; GWR engine cleaner at	m domestic servant ? b&s	Newport, Monmouthshire	50

40

Name	Post	Constit-uency (& dates)	Previous constit-uencies (& dates)	Previous parties (& dates)	Previous Cabinet posts (& dates)	Job(s) prior to politics	Parents; siblings	Place of birth	Age in 1924
Stephen Walsh (1859-1929)	Secretary for War	Ince, Lancs 1906-1929	[Ashton in Makerfield Council 1894-]	?	None	15, fireman at 20; engine driver & TU organiser at 22; ASRS President at 31 and then full-time sec. at 32 miner at 13; TU organiser at 31; VP of MFGB at 63	orphaned as infant; 1b	Liverpool	65
Sidney Webb (1859-1947)	President Board of Trade	Seaham, Durham 1922-1924; Lords as Passfield from 1929	[LCC Cllr, Deptford 1892-1910]	None	None	clerk at 16; civil service at 19; lawyer at 26	f accountant, m hairdresser	London	65
Willie Adamson (1863-1936)	Secretary for Scotland	West Fife 1910-1931	[Dunfermline Council 1905-]	None	None	miner 11-38; TU organiser; President of Fife miners assoc. by 45	f coalminer	Fife	61
John Wheatley (1869-1930)	Minister of Health	Shettleston (Glasgow) 1922-1930	[Lanarkshire CC 1910-1912; then Glasgow City	United Irish League; ILP 1906; formed	None	miner 11-23; shop asst; *Glasgow Observer*	f labourer then miner in Scotland (from 1876);	Co. Waterford, Ireland	55

Name	Post	Constituency (& dates)	Previous constituencies (& dates)	Previous parties (& dates)	Previous Cabinet posts (& dates)	Job(s) prior to politics	Parents; siblings	Place of birth	Age in 1924
			Cllr]	Catholic Socialist Society 1906		advertising copy; publishing company (Hoxton & Walsh) from 39	7 b&s		
Noel Buxton (1869-1948)	Minister of Agriculture	North Norfolk 1922-1930 then Lords as Noel-Buxton	Whitby 1905-1906, North Norfolk 1910-1918 (both as Lib)	Liberal	None	in brewery & charitable work	f director of brewery co., m daughter of Earl of Gainsborough; 9 b&s	London	55
Tom Shaw (1872-1938)	Minister of Labour	Preston 1918-1931	None	None	None	textile factory half-timer at 10; sec. Colne Weavers Assoc; first sec. of Northern Counties Textile Fed.; sec. Int. Fed. of Textile Workers 1911-1929, 1931-1938	f miner; ? b&s	Colne, Lancs.	52
Frederick Roberts (1876-1941)	Minister of Pensions	West Bromwich 1918-1931, 1935-1941	None	?	None	?	?	?	48

42

Name	Post	Constituency (& dates)	Previous constituencies (& dates)	Previous parties (& dates)	Previous Cabinet posts (& dates)	Job(s) prior to politics	Parents; siblings	Place of birth	Age in 1924
Charles Trevelyan (1870-1958)	Minister of Education	Newcastle Central 1922-1931 (having already resigned from 1931 Cabinet)	Elland, Yorks. 1899-1918 (Lib) (joined Labour at end of WWI)	Liberal	(resigned as Liberal Parl. Under-Sec at start of WWI in 1914)	civil servant (at 22?)	f historian, m daughter of Liberal MP; 2 b	London	54
Vernon Hartshorn (1872-1931)	Postmaster General	Ogmore, Glamorgan 1918-1931	None	ILP	None	miner, colliery clerk, checkweighman; miner's agent at 23; MFGB council at 39	f coalminer; ? b&s	Monmouthshire	52
Josiah Wedgwood (1872-1943)	Chancellor of Duchy	Newcastle-under-Lyme 1906-1942 then Lords	None	None	None	shipbuilding 'apprentice'; naval officer; naval architect at 24; Transvaal magistrate at 30	f pottery mfr; ? b&s	Barlaston, N Staffs	52
Fred Jowett (1864-1944)	First Commissioner of Works	East Bradford 1922-1924, 1929-1931 (ILP)	West Bradford 1906-1918 (ILP)	Socialist League 1886; Labour Electoral Alliance	None	textile mill half-timer at 8, full-time at 13; TU organiser	f cotton warp dresser; 7 b&s	Bradford	60

Name	Post	Constit-uency (& dates)	Previous constit-uencies (& dates)	Previous parties (& dates)	Previous Cabinet posts (& dates)	Job(s) prior to politics	Parents; siblings	Place of birth	Age in 1924
Patrick Hastings (1880-1952)	Attorney General	Wallsend 1922-1926 resigned	None	1889; ILP from 1892 Liberal	None	mining engineer; barrister & KC at 39	f solicitor, m painter; 1b	London	44
Henry Slesser (1883-1979)	Solicitor General (not yet MP)	Leeds South East 1924-1929 then law lord in Court of Appeal	None	None	None	LNWR engineering 'apprentice' at 18; barrister at 23; Labour Party counsel at 29	f leather merchant, m concert pianist; ? b&s	London	41
Arthur Henderson (1863-1935)	Home Secretary (not yet MP)	Burnley 1924-1933 Claycross 1933-1935	Barnard Castle 1903-1918; Widnes 1919-1922; Newcastle East 1923-1924	Lib-Lab Cllr and Liberal Party agent	1916	iron-moulder at 12; TU district sec (N'land, Durham, Lancs.) at 29; board of Newcastle Evening News at 31	f weaver, m domestic servant (later married Newcastle policeman 1874); 1b	Glasgow	61

44